INSECT SUPERPOWERS

18 REAL BUGS THAT SMASH, ZAP, HYPNOTIZE, STING, AND DEVOUR!

BY

KATE MESSNER

ILLUSTRATED BY

JILLIAN NICKELL

chronicle books · san francisco

CONTENTS

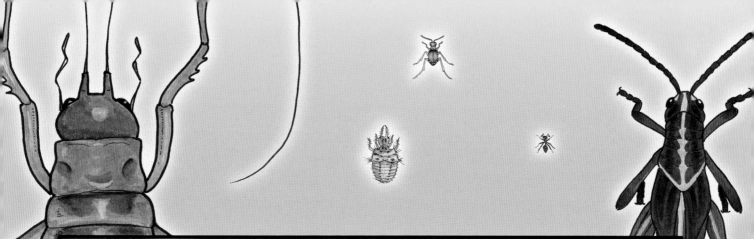

AN INSECT FAMILY TREE

All living organisms are identified using a system called biological classification, where they're organized based on common characteristics. This organization starts big—by asking questions like, "Is it a plant, animal, or something else?"—and gets more specific as it goes along. The levels of classification, from largest to smallest, are: domain, kingdom, phylum, class, order, family, genus, species. The last two categories, genus and species together, make up an organism's scientific name.

Insects are all members of the animal kingdom, along with mammals, birds, and reptiles. They're part of the phylum Arthropoda, which includes not only insects, but also other creatures like spiders, crabs, lobsters, and centipedes. Getting more specific, all insects are part of the class called Insecta.

BLATTODEA-COCKROACHES

INSECT ORDERS

Within the class Insecta are thirty orders with different kinds of insects. Some that you might recognize include:

COLEOPTERA-BEETLE'S

HYMENOPTERA-ANTS, BEES, WASPS

MANTODEA-PRAYING MANTIDS

LEPIDOPTERA-BUTTERFLIES AND MOTHS

DIPTERA-FLIES

5

KINGDOM: ANIMALIA
PHYLUM: ARTHROPODA
CLASS: INSECTA
ORDER: LEPIDOPTERA
FAMILY: NYMPHALIDAE
GENUS: DANAUS
SPECIES: PLEXIPPUS

A MONARCH BUTTERFLY'S SCIENTIFIC NAME IS DANAUS PLEXIPPUS, "DAH-nay-us PLEX-i-pus." IT'S FUN TO SAY. TRY IT!

CHAPTER 1

ROBBER FLY
30-50 MM

FAST & FIERCE

SIX-SPOTTED
TIGER BEETLE
14 MM

WITH SPEEDS THAT PUT OLYMPIC RUNNERS
TO SHAME AND JAWS THAT CAN SLICE
AND DICE IN THE BLINK OF AN EYE, THESE
INSECTS' SUPERPOWERS ARE PERFECT FOR
EVADING PREDATORS AND CATCHING PREY.

ASIAN GIANT
HORNET
UP TO 55 MM QUEEN
35-39 MM WORKER

SUPERSONIC ASSASSIN

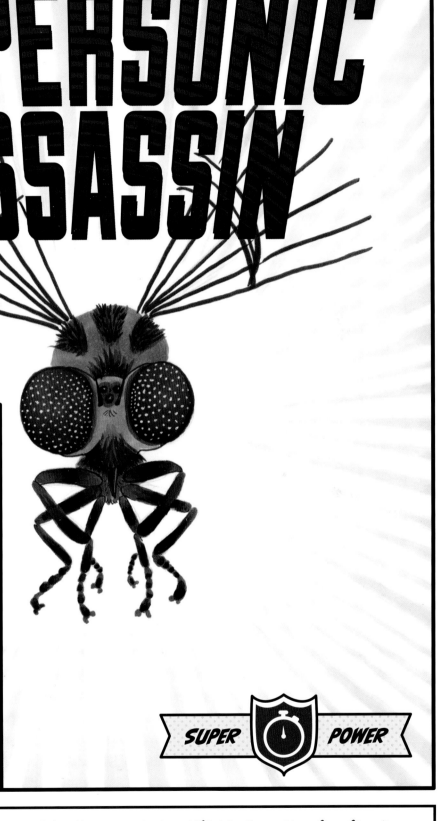

Common Name:
Giant robber fly of the Great Plains

Aliases: Bee killer, assassin fly

Super-Scientific Name:
Microstylum morosum

Trademark Features: Small hollow between the eyes, tufts of hair on the face that may resemble a beard

Size: 30–50 mm

Secret Hideout: Prairies in Texas, Kansas, Oklahoma, and Arkansas

Superpower:
Speed in flight

SUPER ⏱ POWER

Robber flies can fly fast enough to catch other insects in midflight. The robber fly often lies in wait on a twig or leaf where it can see its surroundings and watch for prey. When another insect flies too close—**BUZZ, SWISH, ZAP!**—the robber fly darts out and captures it with long, strong, bristly legs that can hold tight to prey.

The **Japanese beetle** can fly long distances—up to five miles in search of food. But it can't fly fast enough to avoid becoming food for a hungry **robber fly**.

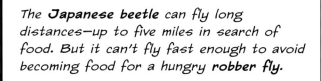

Once the robber fly has another insect in its clutches, it stabs the creature with its hypopharynx and injects saliva into its victim's body. The robber fly's spit contains super-bug chemicals—nerve toxins that paralyze the prey, and digestive enzymes that turn its insides to liquid, which the robber fly then sucks up through its proboscis.

Favorite Food: *Bees, grasshoppers, butterflies, beetles, other robber flies*

Allies: *There are more than seven thousand species of robber flies living all over the world. They're all part of the order Diptera, which includes all flies, and the family Asilidae. Microstylum morosum is the largest robber fly in North America.*

Archenemy: *The eastern kingbird (Tyrannus tyrannus) loves to swoop down from its perch and snap up a juicy robber fly for a meal.*

ARCHENEMY

SLUURRRRP!

Common Name: Asian giant hornet

Alias: Yak killer

Super-Scientific Name: Vespa mandarinia

Trademark Features: Bright-orange head, orange-and-black striped body

Size: 35-39 mm for workers, up to 55 mm for queens.
The Asian giant hornet's stinger alone can be up to 6 mm long.

Secret Hideout: Tree hollows and underground in low mountains and forested areas of Korea, China, Japan, India, and Nepal

Superpower: Fierce jaws and a painful sting

A raiding gang of **Asian giant hornets** has been known to wipe out a nest of tens of thousands of honeybees in a couple of hours.

BZOOOM

The hornets use their powerful mandibles to tear the bees apart, often ripping off heads, legs, and wings. Then the hornets carry the bees' larvae back to the nest, chew them into balls, and feed them to the hornet larvae.

SLASH!

SLURP!

SMACK!

CRUNCH!

But along with that superpower, the Asian giant hornet also has its version of Kryptonite (the one thing that could defeat Superman!).

The hornet's weakness is heat, and **Japanese honeybees** have figured that out. Hornets usually begin a hive raid by sending a scout who marks the spot with chemicals called pheromones.

Sometimes, when that scout shows up at a hive, the Japanese honeybees surround it and start vibrating their bodies to raise the temperature inside the "ball of bees" they've made. The honeybees keep at it until the temperature is about 117°F. The bees can tolerate anything up to 118°F, but the giant hornets don't survive anything over 115°F . . .

. . . so they die inside the cluster of bees and never get the chance to bring back their friends for the raid.

14

Favorite Food: Bees, wasps, beetles, and hornworms

Allies: The Asian giant hornet doesn't really have any friends. It is related to the yellow hornet (Vespa simillima) and its subspecies, the Japanese yellow hornet (Vespa simillima xanthoptera) but the Asian giant hornet often raids the other hornets' nests.

Archenemy: Honey buzzards follow Asian giant hornets back to their nests and feast on them. Scientists aren't entirely sure why the buzzards aren't afraid of the hornets' stings, though some believe the bird's scaly feathers protect it. Others wonder if the honey buzzard might even give off a chemical that repels the hornets.

THE GREEN BOLT

The tiger beetle is the fastest of all the insects. Some can run more than five miles per hour to chase after prey and potential mates. That might not seem superfast, but when you consider the tiger beetle's size, it's pretty impressive.

Common Name: Six-spotted tiger beetle

Alias: Green tiger beetle

Super-Scientific Name: Cicindela sexguttata

Trademark Features: Bright-green body with white spots, sickle-shaped mandibles, and large eyes

Size: Up to 14 mm

Secret Hideout: Burrows in open woods, along paths and streams

Superpower: Speed

TIGER BEETLE MATH

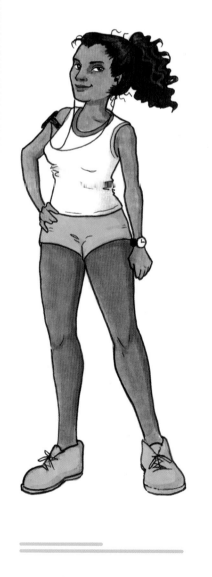

When a **tiger beetle** runs five miles per hour, it's covering about 120 of its body lengths in one second. Let's compare that to the author of this book, who runs about six miles an hour on her morning jog. She's covering about 1.5 of her body lengths per second. To match the relative speed of a tiger beetle, she'd have to run about 480 miles per hour—more than twice the speed of a typical Formula One race car.

In fact, tiger beetles run so fast that they can't see while they're running. The photoreceptors, or light sensors, in their eyes can't take in enough light to create images of the prey they're chasing. Scientists at Cornell University have discovered that tiger beetles use their antennae to sense when there's something in their way. They also stop to look around from time to time while they're chasing prey. Once a tiger beetle relocates its victim, it starts running again and is usually more than fast enough to catch up.

The tiger beetle lurks in a log, waiting for prey. It's quiet and still . . . but not for long!

An unsuspecting ant wanders close . . .

closer . . . then—

ZOOM-SWISH!

CRUNCH!

Allies: There are more than 2,600 species of tiger beetles worldwide. The fastest of them all is *Cicindela hudsoni*, which lives in Australia and can run up to 5.6 miles per hour.

Archenemy: Birds, dragonflies, robber flies (which are superfast in flight!), frogs, and lizards

CHAPTER 2

FIREFLY
20-50 MM

10
20
30

GREAT IMPOSTERS

PINK ORCHID
MANTIS
25-30 MM FOR MALES,
UP TO 60 MM FOR FEMALES

10
20
30

SOME INSECTS HAVE A SUPERPOWER THAT SCIENTISTS CALL MIMICRY: THEY CAN IMITATE ANOTHER ORGANISM, EITHER BY SIGHT OR BY CHEMICAL SMELL. WHETHER THE MIMICKING INSECT DISGUISES ITSELF AS A FLOWER OR ANOTHER BUG, THE RESULTS CAN BE DOWNRIGHT DEADLY.

5

GREEN
LACEWING LARVA
UP TO 12 MM

Common Name: Pink orchid mantis

Alias: Walking flower mantis

Super-Scientific Name: Hymenopus coronatus

Trademark Features: Pink body with leg pieces that stick out and resemble flower petals

Size: Males grow up to 30 mm long, while females can be twice that size. The orchid mantis displays sexual dimorphism, which means that males and females of the species look different from each other.

Secret Hideout: Perched on rainforest plants in Southeast Asia

Superpower: Mimicry

MALEVOLENT MIMIC

The **pink orchid mantis** is a master of mimicry. Perched on a stem or twig, its pink coloration and petal-shaped body parts make it look like one of the delicate orchids of the rainforest. The mantis attaches itself to a plant and sways, waiting for prey.

When a nectar-sipping insect flies too close, the mantis springs into action, seizes the insect in its claws, rips it apart, and feasts. The orchid mantis has been known to tear apart butterflies three times its size.

Scientists who have studied this insect say its pastel color is such a draw that it sometimes attracts more insects than a real flower nearby.

22

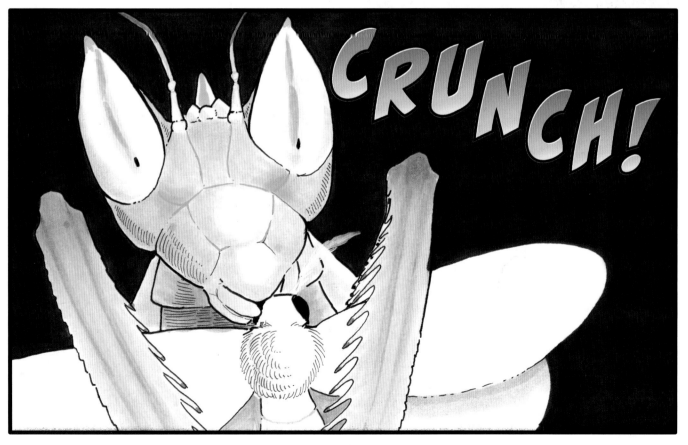

CRUNCH!

This imposter fools people sometimes, too. After returning from a trip in 1879, Australian journalist James Hingston wrote a detailed description of a beautiful orchid that he saw eating insects. Naturalists now believe that was no orchid, but that Hingston had come face-to-face with the orchid mantis.

"I AM TAKEN BY MY KIND HOST AROUND HIS GARDEN, AND SHOWN, AMONG OTHER THINGS, A FLOWER, A RED ORCHID, THAT CATCHES AND FEEDS UPON LIVE FLIES. IT SEIZED UPON A BUTTERFLY WHILE I WAS PRESENT, AND ENCLOSED IT IN ITS PRETTY BUT DEADLY LEAVES, AS A SPIDER WOULD HAVE ENVELOPED IT IN NETWORK."

– JAMES HINGSTON

The Australian Abroad

By James Hingston

Favorite Food: Flies and bees

Allies: The pink orchid mantis is part of a larger family of mantises in the order of insects called Mantodea, with more than 2,400 species.

Archenemy: Birds and lizards prey on the orchid mantis . . . when they can find it. This insect's mimicry skills may also help protect it from predators.

ARCHENEMY

24

APHID IMPOSTER

Common Name: Green lacewing larva

Alias: Trash carrier

Super-Scientific Name: Chrysopa slossonae

Trademark Features: Adult lacewings are pale green with translucent wings, while larvae are often found covered in white woolly material

Size: Up to 12 mm

Secret Hideout: Lurking among woolly alder aphids on alder and silver maple trees east of the Mississippi River

Superpower: Mimicry

SUPER ∞ POWER

The **green lacewing larva** is a master of disguise that dresses up to look like its prey. These larvae have to get past a protector in order to feast on their favorite food, **woolly alder aphids**.

Aphids feed on plant juices, but they don't need much of the plants' carbohydrates, so they excrete these as a substance called honeydew. Ants hang around and wait to drink the honeydew, and in return, they protect the aphids from predators.

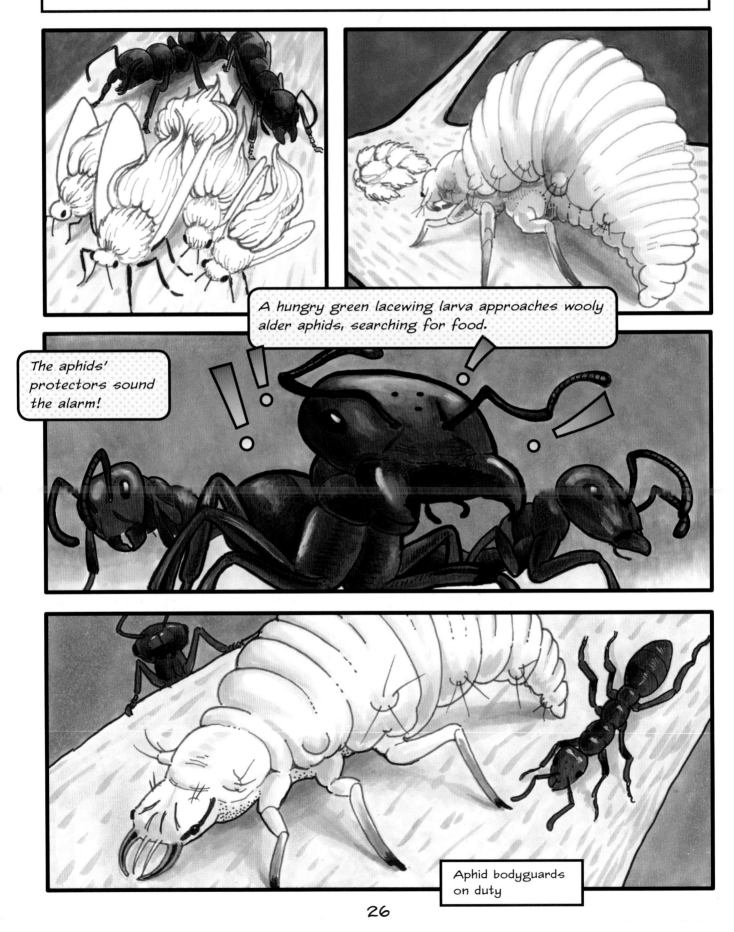

A hungry green lacewing larva approaches wooly alder aphids, searching for food.

The aphids' protectors sound the alarm!

Aphid bodyguards on duty

MASTER OF DISGUISE

The green lacewing larva's solution? A disguise. The larva uses its mandibles as a fork to pull tufts of the aphid's waxy wool from its body. Then the larva twists its body around and plants the wool on its own back. Scientists say it can make itself a convincing aphid costume in less than twenty minutes.

When researchers did studies to find out how well this works, they learned that lacewing larvae without disguises were almost always attacked by the ants, bitten, and literally thrown off the plant. Those with the woolly covering generally slipped by undetected. The ants would poke at them with their antennae and usually leave them alone.

Time to craft a disguise!

TA DA!

APHID

APHID

NOT AN APHID!

APHID

APHID

27

Even the ants that bit the disguised lacewing larvae didn't attack for long. Researchers who studied them report that the ants backed away quickly and then used a leg to wipe the waxy wool from their mouth parts.

ARCHENEMY

Disguised as their own prey, the larvae are free to feed on the woolly alder aphids. They plunge their hollow mandibles into the aphids' bodies and suck out the fluid until the aphids are nothing but woolly husks. The larvae sometimes toss these husks onto their own backs as part of the disguise.

Favorite Food: Woolly alder aphids

Allies: Chrysopa slossonae is one of more than a dozen species of green lacewings in the genus Chrysopa. They're all beneficial insects, so much so that gardeners sometimes use them for pest control.

Archenemy: Birds, bats, and ants that try to keep them from eating aphids

THE FALSE FLASH

Common Name: Firefly

Alias: Lightning bug

Super-Scientific Name:
Photuris versicolor

Trademark Features:
Brown-and-black body

Size: 20-50 mm

Secret Hideout: Meadows,
woods, and yards in the
eastern United States

Superpower: Mimicry

SUPER POWER

All **fireflies** can produce their own light, through a chemical process that happens in their bodies, and that in itself is cool enough. But the female of the species Photuris versicolor can actually flash in a way that imitates a different species of firefly. The goal? Lure in a male with the promise of mating. Then eat him and steal his superpower.

. . . and a male of a DIFFERENT species sees her signal.

Fireflies of the species Photinus ignitus have a special gift of their own. Their bodies contain chemicals called lucibufagins, which taste awful and help to deter predators like birds and spiders. Photuris versicolor doesn't have that chemical naturally, so the only way it can get it is by eating the other species.

He answers with a light signal of his own—and the female flashes back. Will she be his perfect mate?

Fireflies flash their lights when they're looking for a mate. Each species has its own particular pattern of long and short flashes—sort of like a Morse code that male fireflies use to signal to females. Female fireflies answer with a single flash, carefully timed. The males identify females of their own species by the length of time it takes them to answer. When they do, they fly to the female to mate.

But female fireflies of the Photuris versicolor species send out different kinds of light signals—one to attract their own species for mating and one to attract the males of Photinus ignitus, for eating. When a male firefly of that other species answers the call, the female firefly overpowers him and eats him.

The answer is no.

Male fireflies may think they're about to mate. In reality, they've been chosen for a different kind of "dinner date"—

The female not only gets a nice meal, but also acquires those protective chemicals from the blood of the male of the other species. These chemicals protect the female firefly from predators like birds and spiders, and she's also able to pass on that chemical protection to her eggs, so ants don't eat them.

—one where THEY'RE the dinner.

ARCHENEMY

Favorite Food: Insects, slugs, mites, other fireflies

Allies: There are more than two thousand species of fireflies worldwide.

Archenemy: Spiders and birds

31

CHAPTER 3

IRONCLAD
BEETLE
UP TO 29 MM

BIG & TOUGH

WE THINK OF INSECTS AS SMALL ANIMALS,
BUT SOME ARE IMPRESSIVELY LARGE—
AND THESE BIG BUGS ARE AMONG THE
ROUGHEST, TOUGHEST, STRONGEST
CREATURES ON EARTH. IT'S TIME TO MEET
OUR HEAVYWEIGHT CHAMPS!

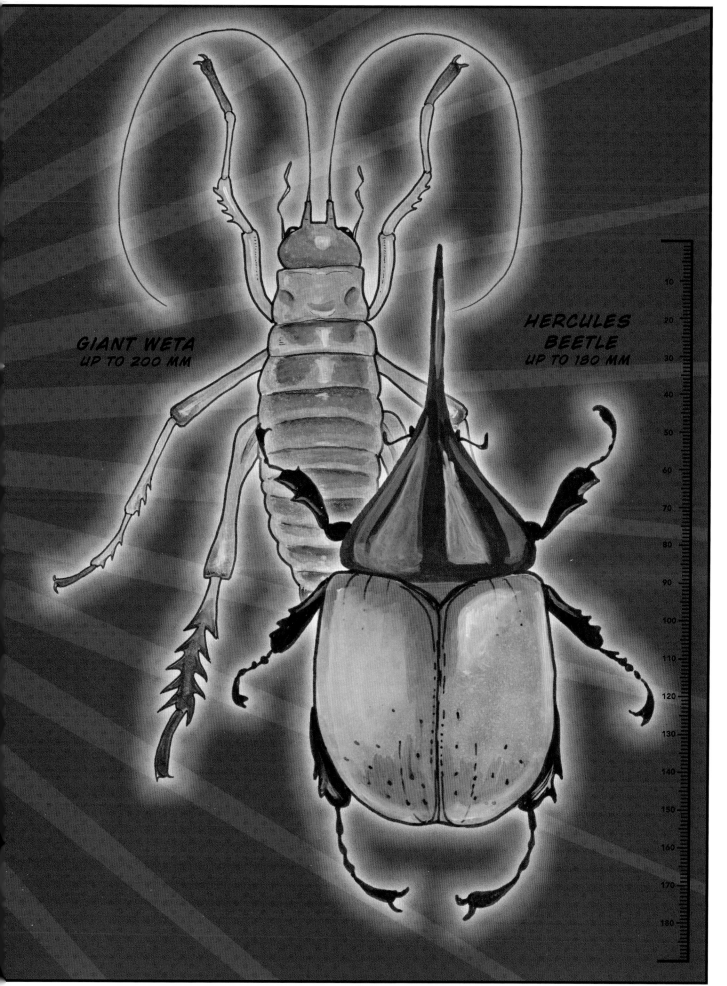

GIANT WETA
UP TO 200 MM

HERCULES
BEETLE
UP TO 180 MM

SUPER 🛡 POWER

Common Name:
Hercules beetle

Alias: Rhinoceros beetle

Super-Scientific Name:
Dynastes hercules

Trademark Features:
Green/black body with
a long double horn

Size: Up to 180 mm

Secret Hideout:
Moist forests and
cloud forests in
Central and South
America

Superpower:
Heavyweight lifting!
Throwing competitors!

THE WEIGHT LIFTER

The **Hercules beetle** is known for its superstrength. It's supposedly able to lift 850 times its body weight. By comparison, elite human weight lifters can sometimes lift twice their own body weight.

Male Hercules beetles most often use their strength to fight with one another over females and feeding territory, sometimes lifting and throwing each other with their horns.

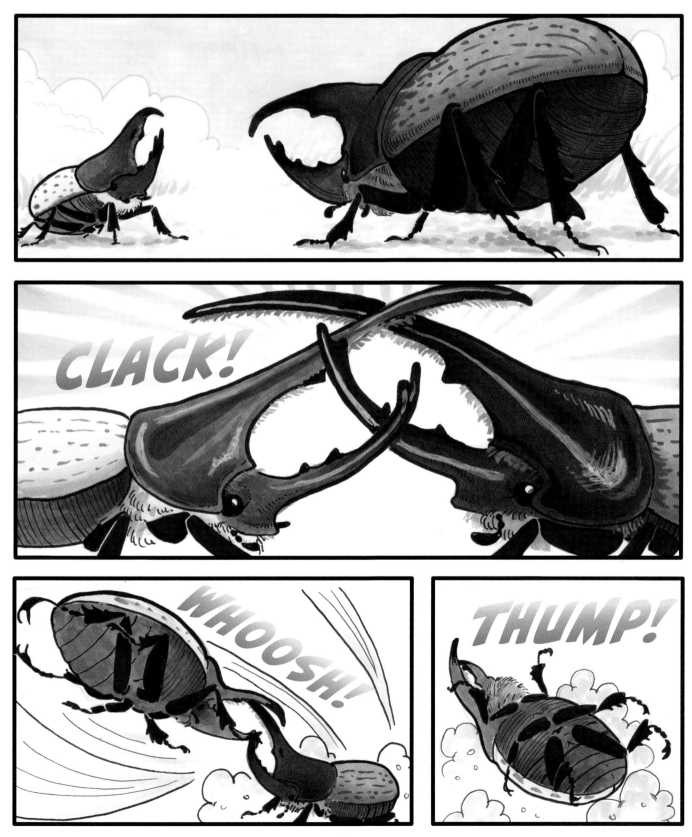

Allies: The Hercules beetle's closest relatives include another insect with heavy lifting abilities—the dung beetle, which, like the Hercules beetle, also belongs to the family Scarabaeoidea. The dung beetle uses its strength to roll up dung into round balls, which it then uses as a food source.

Favorite Food: Rotting fruit and wood

Archenemy: Birds, rats, bats, and some reptiles

ARCHENEMY

THE MUTANT GRASSHOPPER

Common Name: Little Barrier Island giant weta

Alias: Wetapunga—sometimes translated from Maori as "god of ugly things."

Super-Scientific Name: Deinacrida heteracantha

Trademark Features: Large, round, brown bodies with spiny legs

Size: Up to 100 mm body length with up to a 200 mm leg span! The heaviest giant weta on record was a female that weighed 71 grams, but that's unusually large. Most giant wetas can grow to about 35 grams. That's still heavier than a typical mouse or sparrow.

Secret Hideout: Among dead foliage—drooping leaves and curled-up fern fronds—in New Zealand

Superpower: Super big and super ugly

The **Little Barrier Island giant weta** is the **heaviest insect in the world**—so large that it used to fill the ecological role of small rodents, thriving throughout New Zealand, before non-native people arrived and introduced rats that had stowed away on their boats.

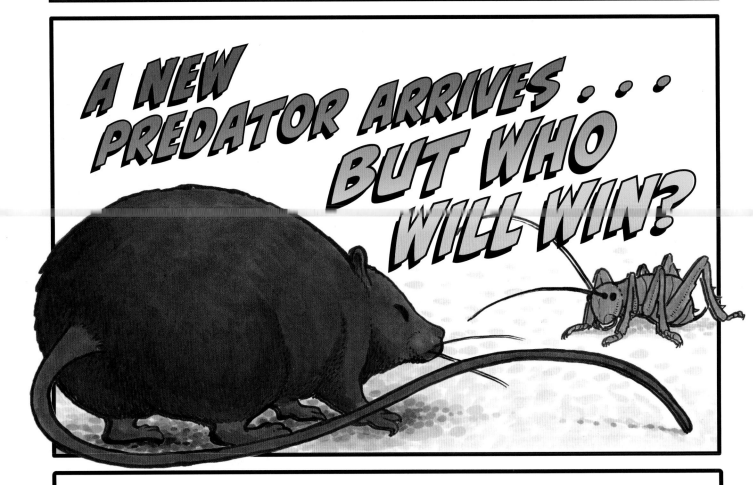

After rats were introduced, the giant weta died out on most of the islands. Now, it only survives naturally on Little Barrier Island. However, New Zealand's government has been running a program to breed and release giant wetas on other predator-free islands, so that their survival as a species doesn't depend on just that one island's population.

The giant weta has no wings, so it can't fly, and it's too slow and heavy to jump, so it relies on its massive size and scary looks to deter predators. When threatened, giant wetas sometimes raise their spiky hind legs in the air as a warning.

After feasting on leaves, a giant weta descends from the tree.

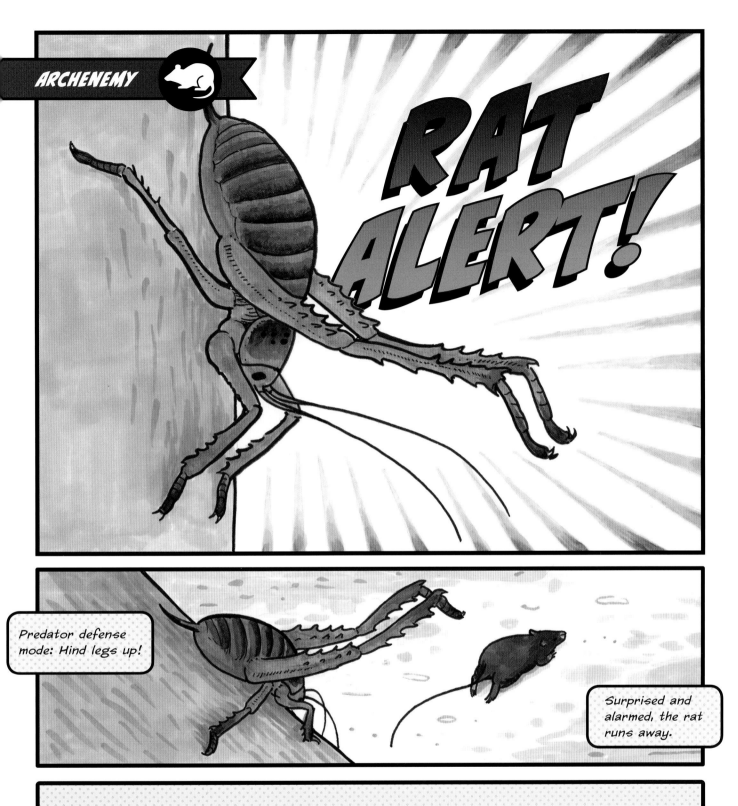

RAT ALERT!

Predator defense mode: Hind legs up!

Surprised and alarmed, the rat runs away.

Favorite Food: Leaves of the karaka and karamu trees

Allies: There are eleven species of giant weta in New Zealand. The Little Barrier Island giant weta is the largest. These insect giants are among the oldest in the world. Scientists in Queensland have discovered fossil wetas from 190 million years ago.

Archenemy: The kiore (Pacific rat) as well as the morepork (Tasmanian spotted owl), harriers, and kingfishers

SHELL OF STEEL

Common Name: Texas Ironclad beetle

Alias: Another beetle, Asbolus verrucosus, shares the nickname ironclad beetle but is also called the blue death-feigning beetle.

Super-Scientific Name: Zopherus nodulosus haldemani

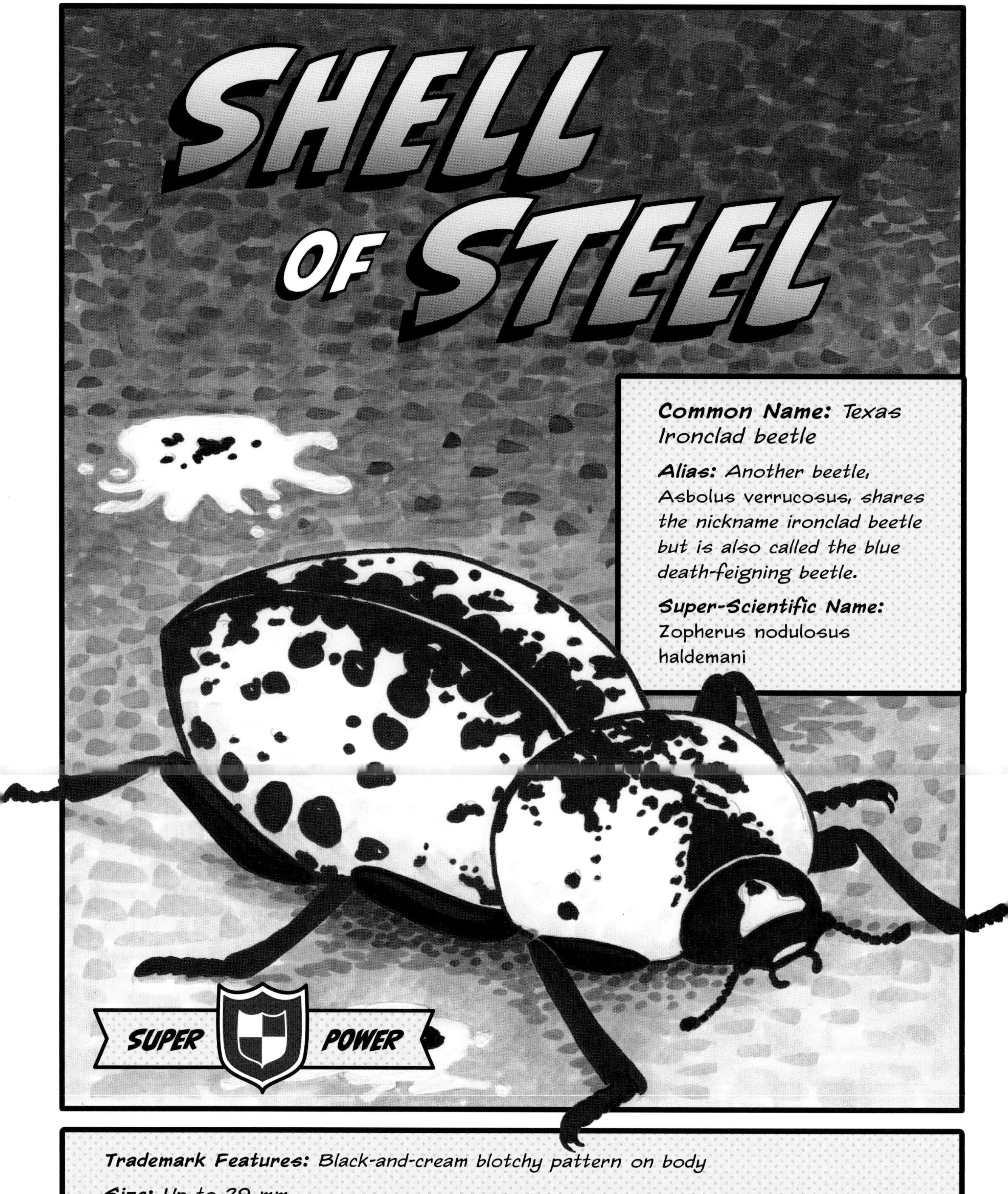

SUPER POWER

Trademark Features: Black-and-cream blotchy pattern on body

Size: Up to 29 mm

Secret Hideout: Pecan and oak trees in the southwestern United States and Mexico

Superpower: Super-tough exoskeleton

The ironclad beetle's power is its armor—a super-tough exoskeleton that protects it from most predators. When threatened, these beetles tuck in their legs and play dead. **With their mottled black-and-white coloring, they resemble bird droppings.**

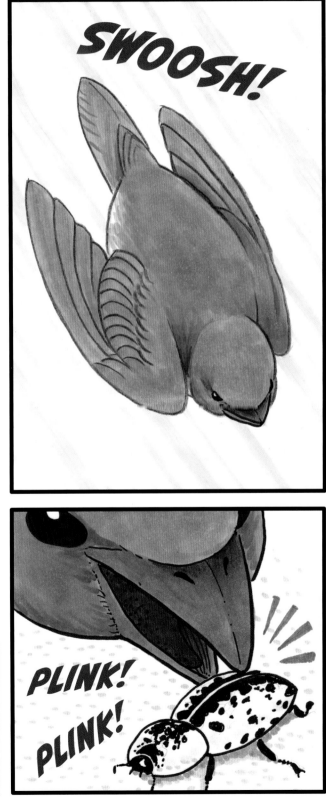

SWOOSH!

PLINK!
PLINK!

If predators aren't deterred by the beetle's appearance, most can't get through its tough shell. Even when an ironclad beetle is dead, researchers and bug collectors often need a drill to puncture its shell.

Ironclad beetles have such tough exoskeletons that living beetles are sometimes decorated with gems and used as jewelry in Mexico. In 2010, a woman tried to pass through United States Customs and Border Patrol with a living, bejeweled ironclad beetle pinned to her sweater. She didn't have the correct paperwork for her pet/jewelry and was not allowed to bring it into the United States.

ARCHENEMY

Favorite Food: Lichen that's often found on pecan and oak trees

Allies: The Texas ironclad beetle is one of nineteen species in this genus, though none of the others resemble the Texas beetle in appearance.

Archenemy: Birds and reptiles prey on most insects and might like to eat ironclad beetles, too, but the beetle's hard shell usually protects it.

CHAPTER 4

TERMITE
4-5 MM

MASTERS OF CHEMICAL WEAPONRY

BOMBARDIER BEETLE
UP TO 20 MM

LUBBER GRASSHOPPER
(UP TO 60 MM (MALE))
UP TO 80 MM (FEMALE)

WHAT IF INSECTS WERE THE SIZE OF PEOPLE? THAT WOULD BE PRETTY SCARY TO BEGIN WITH. BUT NOW IMAGINE A HUMAN-SIZE TERMITE WITH A GOO GUN FOR A FACE, OR A BEETLE THE SIZE OF A BEAR THAT SCUTTLES ALONG SHOOTING A HOT, TOXIC CHEMICAL MIST FROM ITS BOTTOM! THESE ARE THE INSECT WORLD'S MASTERS OF CHEMICAL WEAPONS.

MACHINE GUN BUTT

POP! POP! POP!

SUPER POWER

Common Name: African bombardier beetle

Alias: Bull's-eye beetle

Super-Scientific Name: Stenaptinus insignis

Trademark Features: Orange-and-black coloring

Size: Up to 20 mm

Secret Hideout: Damp areas under logs, bark, and rocks

Superpower: Firing a hot chemical spray out its rear end

USA 33

Bombardier beetle

One species of bombardier beetle had a moment of fame in 1999 when the U.S. Postal Service put it on a stamp.

Sneak up on a bombardier beetle, and you're likely to get burned. This beetle has an amazing defense mechanism—the ability to spray a **hot, noxious mist from its abdomen.** The bombardier beetle has a reservoir inside its body where it stores chemicals called hydroquinones and hydrogen peroxide.

Those two substances don't normally interact with each other unless they come into contact with a special kind of enzyme. An enzyme is a substance that causes a chemical reaction, and the bombardier beetle just happens to have that special enzyme, stored in another secret hiding place, called **the reaction chamber.**

When something bothers a bombardier beetle, it compresses its chemical reservoir to send the contents into that reaction chamber, where the two substances mix with the enzyme, and then . . . **POP!** An **actual explosion** takes place, and the superhot chemical mixture **blasts out the beetle's rear end** at the attacker. This actually happens in a series of superfast pulses—five hundred to one thousand per second, scientists have learned! So the bombardier beetle's defense is sort of **like a hot chemical machine gun.**

Favorite Food: Insects, including other bombardier beetles and larvae

Allies: There are many different kinds of bombardier beetles, all part of the class Insecta, the order Coleoptera (beetles), and the family Carabidae (ground beetles). Worldwide, there are more than five hundred species of bombardier beetles living on every continent except Antarctica.

There's a famous story about Charles Darwin's encounter with a bombardier beetle. Darwin writes that he was out collecting beetles one day and had one in each hand when he saw a third, different kind. So what did he do? He tried to put one in his mouth for safekeeping, then wrote about it in his autobiography . . .

"I popped the one which I held in my right hand into my mouth. Alas! It ejected some intensely acrid fluid, which burnt my tongue so that I was forced to spit the beetle out, which was lost, as was the third one."

Archenemy: Ants, spiders, frogs, and birds would all love to eat the bombardier beetle, but it can often fight them off with its defensive spray. But the cane toad (Bufo marinus) in Central and South America has found a way to overcome that. It swallows its local species of bombardier beetle in one gulp, before it has a chance to spray. Scientists have even heard the beetle giving off muffled popping noises from inside the toad's stomach.

THE VOMITIZER

Common Name: Lubber grasshopper

Alias: Eastern lubber grasshopper, southeastern lubber grasshopper

Super-Scientific Name: Romalea microptera

Trademark Features: Large yellow-and-black bodies

Size: Up to 60 mm for males, 80 mm for females

Secret Hideout: Open pine woods, roadsides, and weedy fields in the southeastern and south-central United States

Superpower: Vomiting

SUPER POWER

The *eastern lubber grasshopper* actually has a *collection* of superpowers that helps keep it safe from enemies.

When threatened, the grasshopper first displays its bright rose-colored hind wings as a warning. Predators who don't back away may then be poked by **sharp spines** on the grasshopper's hind legs. And if that's not enough of a deterrent, the grasshopper starts **spraying** and **puking** noxious liquids.

It's the Vomitizer's nemesis: the LOGGERHEAD SHRIKE!

The grasshopper springs into action—

—releasing repulsive fluids and a nasty hiss!

HISSSSS

SQUAWK!

The grasshopper makes a loud hissing sound when it sprays a chemical mist from a gland in its thorax, and it also regurgitates a dark-brown fluid. That liquid is pretty offensive to other animals, thanks to some of the bitter plants that make up the grasshopper's diet.

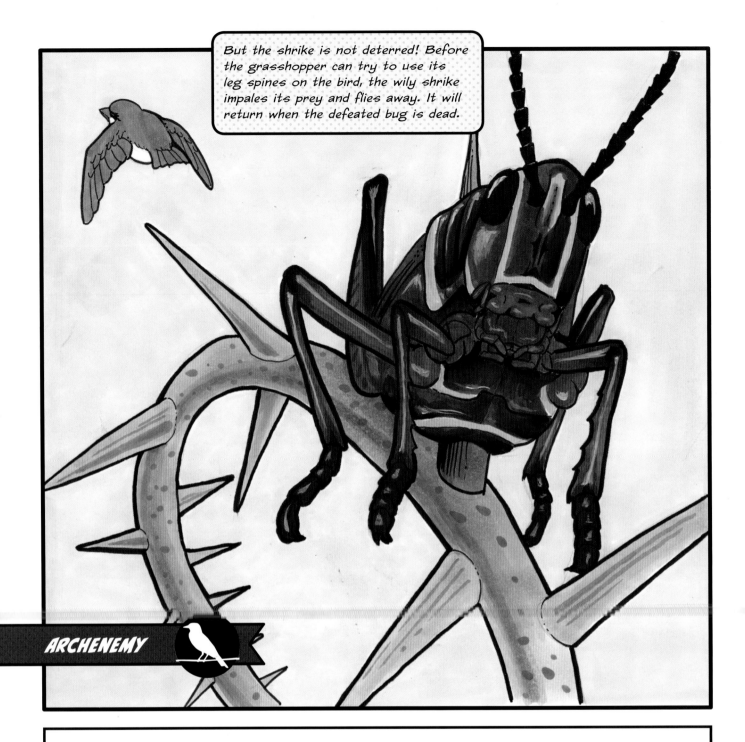

But the shrike is not deterred! Before the grasshopper can try to use its leg spines on the bird, the wily shrike impales its prey and flies away. It will return when the defeated bug is dead.

ARCHENEMY

But a few predators have found ways to get around that. Some birds bite off the grasshopper's head first. One bird, the loggerhead shrike, has actually been observed impaling the grasshoppers on sharp plant thorns and coming back to eat them in a day or two, when there's no longer a danger of being sprayed or puked on.

Favorite Food: Grasshoppers eat a wide variety of plant material but especially love flowering plants and citrus trees, which makes them a real pest in Florida.

Allies: Eastern lubber grasshoppers are part of the family called Romaleidae, which includes more than two hundred species.

Archenemy: Birds, especially the loggerhead shrike

THE GREAT GLUE SHOOTER

Common Name: Termite

Alias: White ant

Super-Scientific Name:
Nasutitermes exitiosus

SUPER POWER

Trademark Features: Soldiers have round, dark-brown heads with long snouts

Size: 4–5 mm

Secret Hideout: In dome-shaped nests in Australia

Superpower: Shooting smelly glue from a gun on its face

READY . . . AIM . . . FIRE! A TERMITE SHOOTS GLUE FROM ITS FACE TO FEND OFF AN ATTACKING ANT.

Nasutitermes exitiosus is a termite with a superpowered weapon—a **smelly glue gun** in its snout. Soldiers of this species have glands in their snouts that produce a stinky, sticky chemical goo. When the termite soldiers are attacked, they turn their heads, then squirt out this fluid as a thin filament that can be several times the length of their own bodies. This sticky loop both irritates and immobilizes their enemies.

A hungry ant searches for prey . . .

and finds a termite, BUT—

Pshhheww!

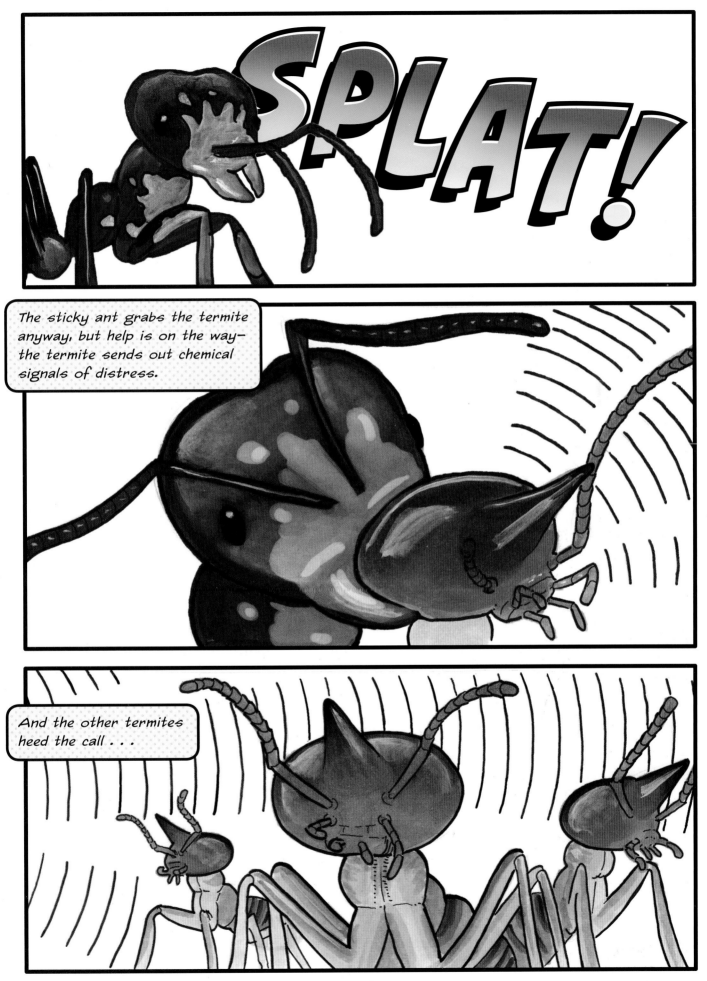

The sticky ant grabs the termite anyway, but help is on the way—the termite sends out chemical signals of distress.

And the other termites heed the call . . .

Scientists say the sticky substance also seems to contain pheromones—chemicals that signal other termite soldiers to come help ward off the attacker.

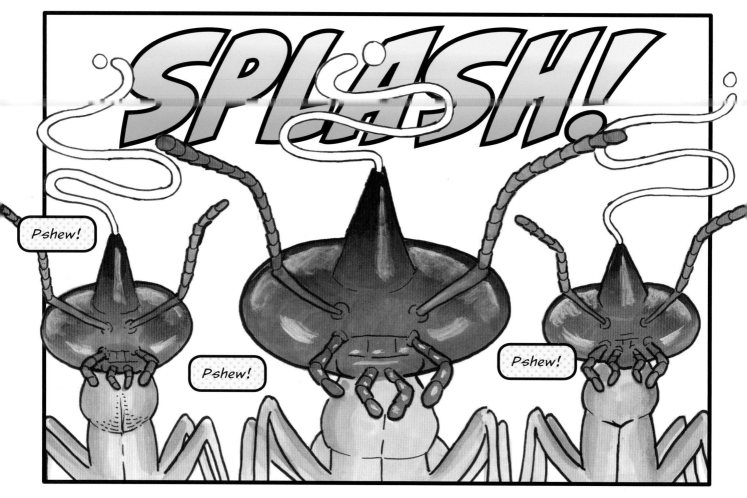

Favorite Food: Wood. Termites are known as pests because they eat both living wood and wood in buildings.

Allies: Nasutitermes exitiosus is believed to be a descendant of cockroaches that evolved so they could eat wood. It's part of the order Isoptera, which includes over two thousand species.

Archenemy: Ants, spiders, and centipedes

CHAPTER 5

HAWK MOTH
90–130 MM (WINGSPAN)

90 80 70 60 50 40 30 20 10

ENGINEERS & ARCHITECTS

LEAF-CUTTER ANT
UP TO 22 MM (QUEEN)
UP TO 14 MM (WORKER ANT)

10

ANTLION
15 MM

10

INSECTS MAY NOT HAVE BIG BRAINS COMPARED WITH PEOPLE, BUT SOME OF THEM HAVE DEVELOPED SUPER SKILLS AS ENGINEERS AND ARCHITECTS. IN THIS CHAPTER, YOU'LL MEET A FARMER-ARCHITECT, A BUILDER OF EVIL LAIRS, AND A MOTH WITH MILITARY-LEVEL SONAR-JAMMING SKILLS.

THE EVIL ARCHITECT

The antlion gets its "doodlebug" nickname from the designs it makes in the sand. But really, this sand art is the result of the antlion's search for the perfect spot to build a CLEVER PIT OF DOOM!

SUPER POWER

Common Name: Antlion

Alias: Doodlebug

Super-Scientific Name: Myrmeleon carolinus

Trademark Features: Flat head with sickle-shaped jaws; plump, round abdomen

Size: Most North American antlion larvae grow to be about 15 mm long.

Secret Hideout: Under leaves and wood, in sandy pits, wherever there's sand

Superpower: Building elaborate traps for prey

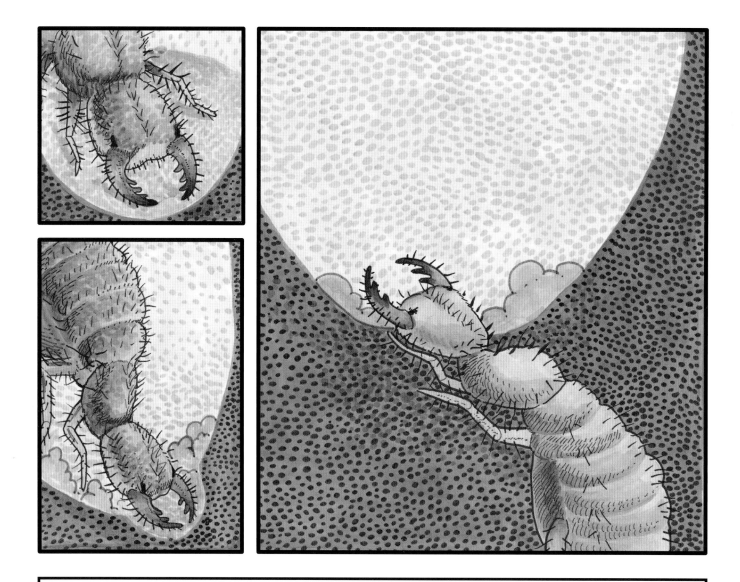

The **antlion larva** is a master architect. It digs a funnel-shaped pit in sandy soil, then waits at the bottom with only its head exposed.

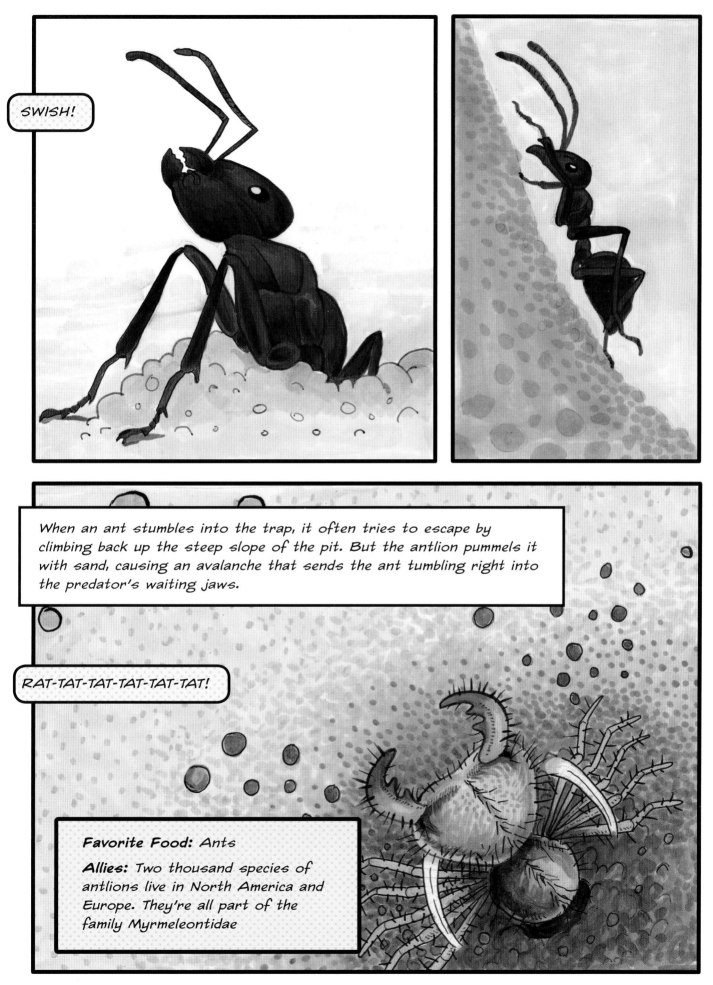

SWISH!

When an ant stumbles into the trap, it often tries to escape by climbing back up the steep slope of the pit. But the antlion pummels it with sand, causing an avalanche that sends the ant tumbling right into the predator's waiting jaws.

RAT-TAT-TAT-TAT-TAT-TAT!

Favorite Food: Ants

Allies: Two thousand species of antlions live in North America and Europe. They're all part of the family Myrmeleontidae

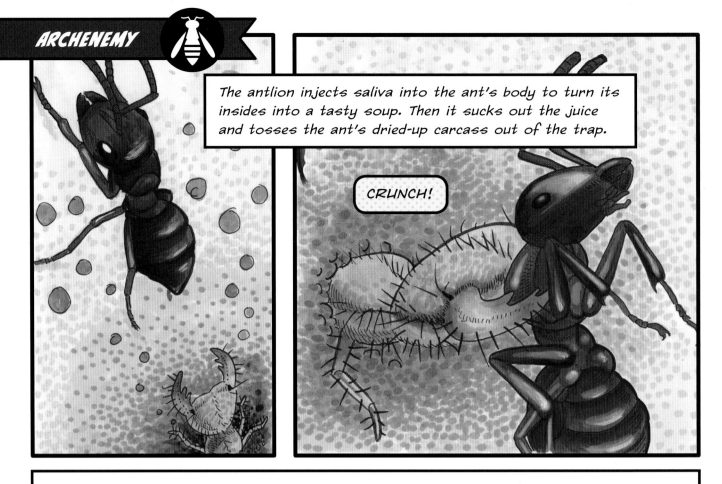

The antlion injects saliva into the ant's body to turn its insides into a tasty soup. Then it sucks out the juice and tosses the ant's dried-up carcass out of the trap.

CRUNCH!

Some antlions can even eat ants that have their own superpower defenses. Scientists did an experiment with the ant called Camponotus floridanus, which can spray acid when it clamps onto an attacker with its mandibles. They found that the antlion was able to outsmart its prey by attacking it in a way that didn't trigger the acidic spray and then sucking the juice from the ant's body without puncturing the acid sack.

Archenemy: The antlion's master building skills can also be its downfall. Birds sometimes spot the sandy traps and know they can swoop in to pluck out a meal. Antlions are also prey to a kind of parasitic chalcid wasp. The wasp tricks the antlion into grabbing its legs, then takes that opportunity to inject its eggs into a membrane of the antlion's throat. When the eggs hatch, the wasp larvae eat the antlion from the inside out.

THE
FUNGUS FARMER

Common Name:
Leaf-cutter ant

Alias: *Parasol ant*

Super-Scientific Name: Atta cephalotes

SUPER ⚫ POWER

Trademark Features: Reddish colored with three pairs of spines on the thorax (to help with carrying leaf bits on their backs)

Size: Up to 14 mm for workers, 22 mm for queens.

Secret Hideout: Clearings and forest edges in Central and South America

Superpower: Superstrength, super organization, and super farming skills

Workers use their powerful jaws to cut leaf fragments.

They carry these on a march through the forest, back to the colony.

The **leaf-cutter** ant has some **seriously impressive superpowers.**

The ants don't eat the leaves; they use them to farm the fungus they grow as food for the colony. When the worker ants return to the nest, smaller workers chew up those leaf bits into a paste that fertilizes the fungus.

While the rooms in your house are used for cooking and sleeping, most of the ants' chambers serve as fungus gardens. Others are for storing garbage—everything from dead ants to old, used-up leaves.

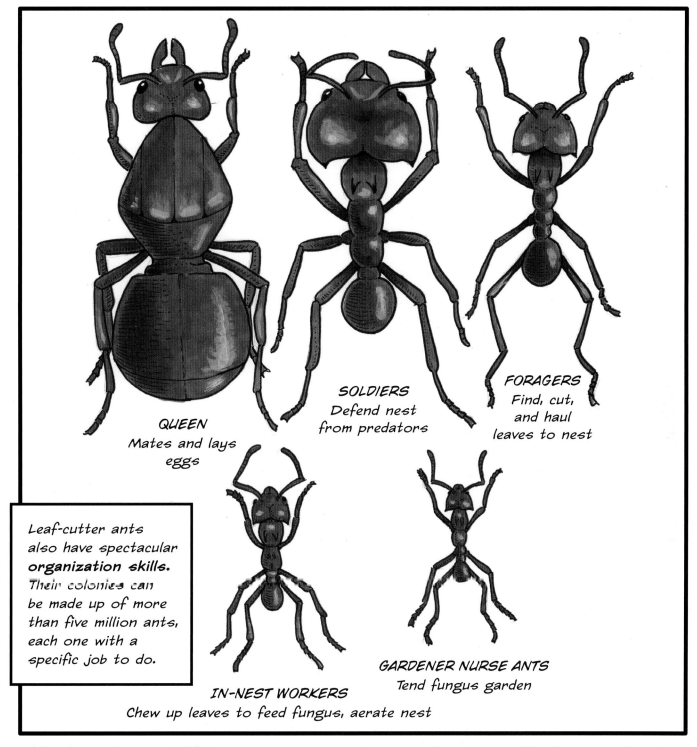

QUEEN
Mates and lays eggs

SOLDIERS
Defend nest from predators

FORAGERS
Find, cut, and haul leaves to nest

IN-NEST WORKERS
Chew up leaves to feed fungus, aerate nest

GARDENER NURSE ANTS
Tend fungus garden

Leaf-cutter ants also have spectacular **organization skills.** Their colonies can be made up of more than five million ants, each one with a specific job to do.

Large **soldier ants** guard the colony while smaller ants work in the fungus garden, fertilizing and clearing away waste to a special garbage chamber in the colony. Other ants go out and use their **powerful jaws** to cut and carry leaves. These are mostly larger workers, but some smaller ants go out on leaf-cutting trips and then hitch a lift back to the colony on the leaf being carried by another ant. Scientists don't think these ants are actually hitchhiking. Instead, they're acting as **bodyguards** to protect the carrying ant from parasitic flies.

Favorite Food: Fungus

Allies: Atta cephalotes is one of more than three dozen species of leaf-cutter ants.

Archenemy: Armadillos and anteaters (Uh-oh, here comes an anteater now . . .)

ARCHENEMY

Slurp! Smack!

THE SONAR SMASHER

Common Name: Yam hawk moth

Alias: Hummingbird moth

Super-Scientific Name: Theretra nessus

Trademark Features: Light- and dark-brown wings, gold stripes on each side of abdomen, long proboscis

Size: Wingspan 90-130 mm

Secret Hideout: Jungles of Southeast Asia

Superpower: Super sounds for sonar jamming

The **hawk moth** takes advantage of the fact that bats have a superpower of their own— **echolocation**. Insect-eating bats hunt at night, so to find their prey, they emit sounds and listen for the echoes of those sounds to bounce back. Those echoes help the bats to identify and locate possible meals (like the hawk moth!).

BUT. . .

CHIRP! CHIRP!

Scientists have discovered that when some kinds of hawk moths are exposed to bat sonar sounds, they make a **defensive chirping sound** of their own by rubbing their genitals against their abdomens.

The researchers believe these sounds may warn bats away and **interfere with the bats' echolocation** abilities so that they can't identify or locate the hawk moths.

CHIRP! CHIRP!

Favorite Food: The hawk moth sips nectar with its long proboscis.

The hawk moth is such an important pollinator that some plants can't survive without it.

ARCHENEMY

Allies: There are more than 1,400 species of hawk moths around the world, though only a few have been shown to have the sonar-jamming superpower so far. Two other insects, tiger moths and tiger beetles, are also believed to give off noises that interfere with bats' sonar.

Archenemy: Bats

SUPER-STING

Common Name: Bullet ant

Alias: Conga ant, lesser giant hunting ant, 24-hour ant

Super-Scientific Name: Paraponera clavata

Trademark Features: Reddish-black body, looks like a wasp without wings

If you get stung, that's how long you'll feel the pain.

Favorite Food: Small insects and nectar

SUPER POWER

Size: One of the world's largest ants, the bullet ant can grow to be about 25 mm long.

Secret Hideout: Nests at the bases of rainforest trees in Central and South America

Superpower: The most painful insect sting in the world

Bullet ants aren't usually aggressive unless their colony is being disturbed. Then, watch out! A small army of defenders will **swarm out** to fend off the intruders. Bullet ants grab victims with their mandibles to hold them still while they **plunge in their stingers** to deliver venom. The neurotoxin delivered by this sting causes not only **extreme pain**, but also **muscle spasms** and **temporary paralysis**.

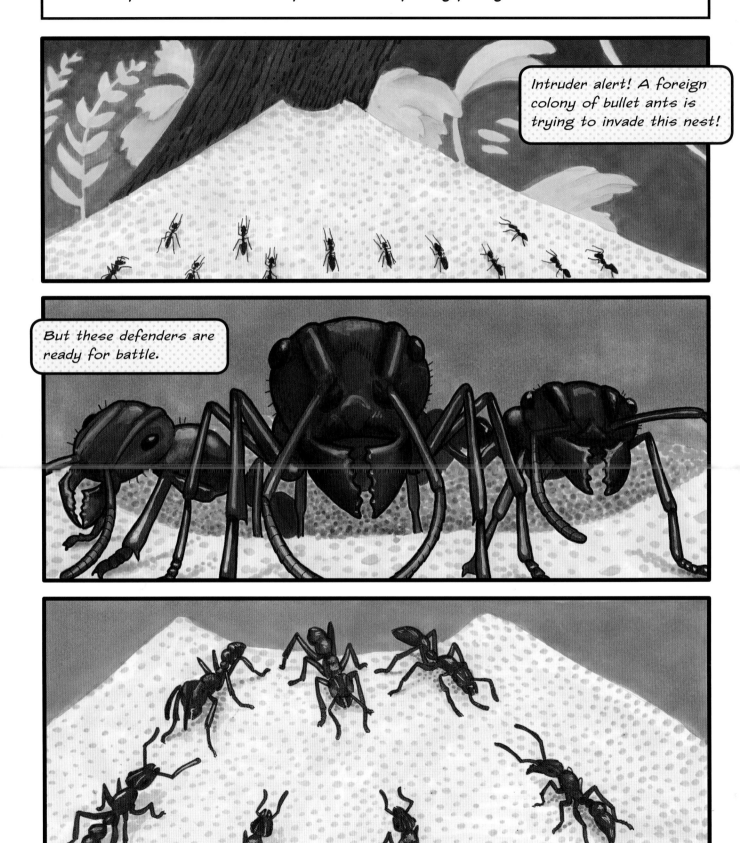

Intruder alert! A foreign colony of bullet ants is trying to invade this nest!

But these defenders are ready for battle.

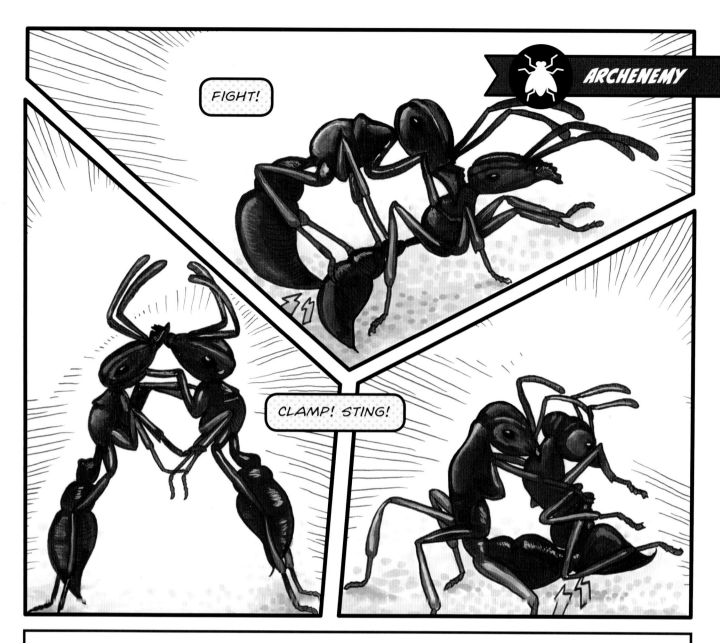

One tribe in Brazil uses bullet ants as part of its initiation ceremony for warriors. Tribe members submerge the ants in a mixture of herbs to make them unconscious; then they **weave the knocked-out ants into a glove** of leaves, with their **stingers pointing inward**. The young man hoping to be a warrior must put his hands into the gloves and wear them for several minutes, enduring stings that are said to **feel like bullets**. According to National Geographic, he's required to go through the entire painful ceremony numerous times before being accepted as a warrior.

Allies: The bullet ant is one of only two known species of ants in the genus Paraponera. The other one, Paraponera dieteri, is extinct, but a specimen more than fifteen million years old was found preserved in amber.

Archenemy: Bullet ants don't have many enemies willing to take on the risk of that painful sting. However, they do sometimes fall prey to a small insect called the phorid fly. About the size of a fruit fly, the phorid fly is attracted to the scent of worker ants when they're injured. The female phorid fly often lays eggs on the injured bullet ant, and both male and female flies land on it and use it as a food source.

Common Name: Slave-making ant

Alias: Pirate ant

Super-Scientific Name: Polyergus breviceps

SUPER POWER

No. That's not why they're called pirate ants.

Trademark Features: Red coloring

Size: 4-7 mm

Secret Hideout: Under rocks and around shade trees in the western United States.

Superpower: Forcing other ants to do their work

THE PIRATE QUEEN

The pirate ant doesn't rear its own young, forage for its own food, or clean its own nests. This species is what scientists call helotistic, which means that it **forces other ants** to do the work needed to sustain its colony. Pirate ants have two different ways of accomplishing this. Sometimes, the worker ants go out to raid neighboring colonies, most often of the species Formica gnava or Formica occulta. These raiders invade the other nest, steal its larvae, and carry them back to the original nest. When those larvae emerge, they learn the smell of the new nest and work as if they've been part of that colony all along, grooming and feeding the queen and the larvae, foraging for dead insects, and clearing the nest of discarded fly wings and other debris.

Slave-making ants raid other ants' nests and enlist the residents as workers. Here, a red pirate ant watches over workers of another species hauling old insect wings out of the nest.

Pirate ants also **raid other nests** when they need to establish new colonies. In this situation, the original colony might send a new queen out on a raid along with the workers. The pirate queen invades the host nest, **hunts down its queen, kills her,** and **steals her smell.** Scientists believe this takeover happens thanks to pheromones, special chemicals that trigger a response in members of the same species. They believe the pirate queen acquires pheromones while she's biting and licking the host queen's body during the attack. Once the old queen is dead, the worker ants of the nest recognize the new queen as their own.

Formica gnava *nest*

In a nearby Formica gnava nest, ants are going about their day . . . unaware that a RAID is about to BEGIN!

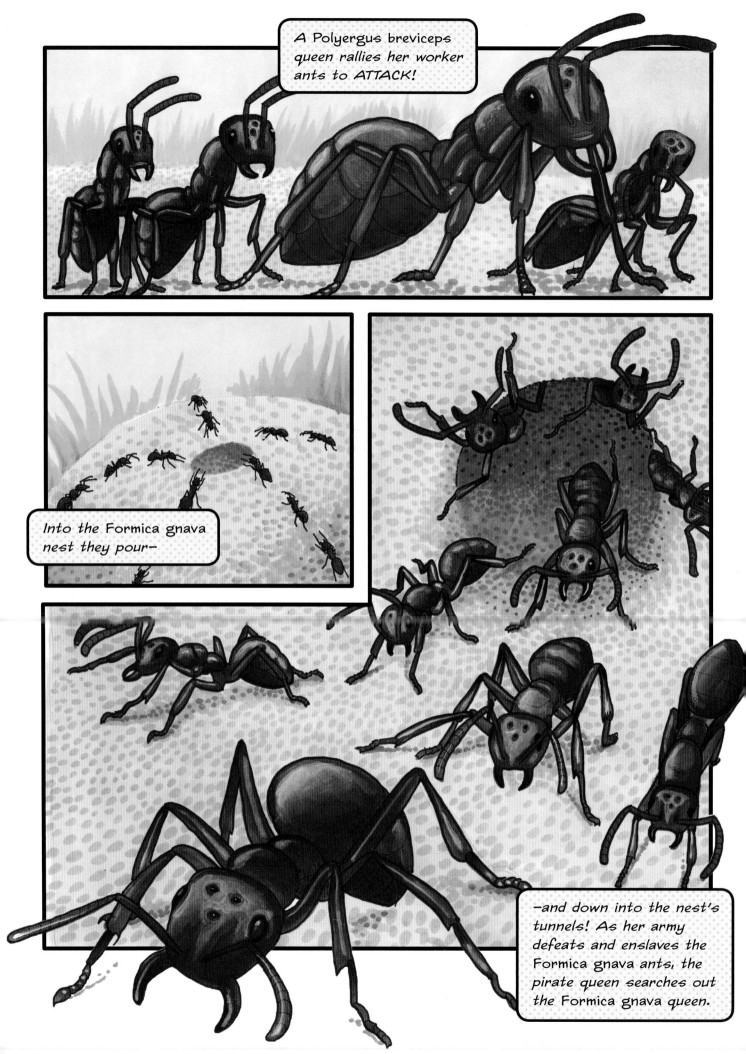

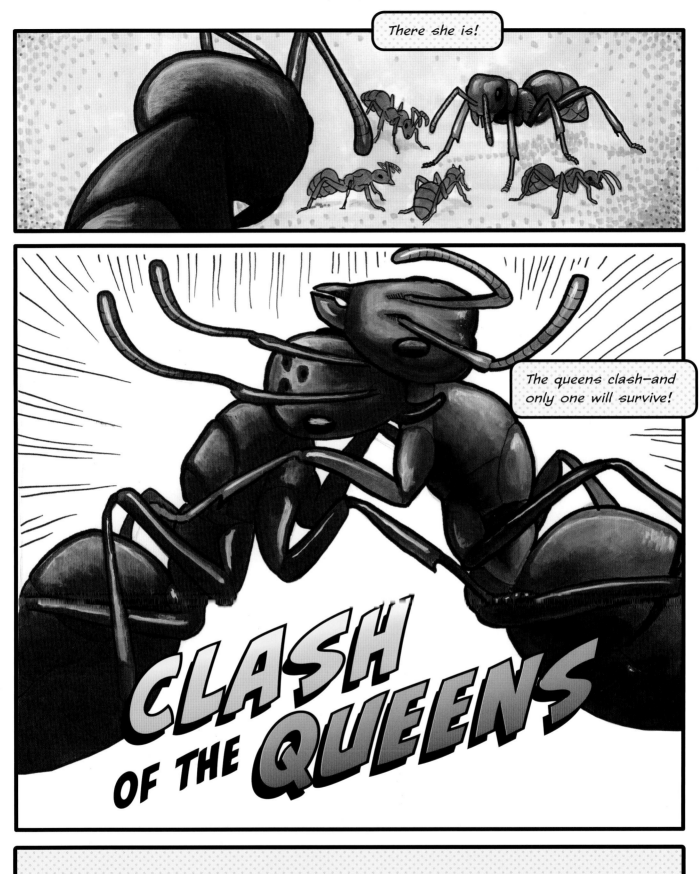

Favorite Food: Dead insects and nectar

Allies: More than a dozen different species of ants in the Polyergus genus carry out this kind of raid. Other ants that show similar behaviors belong to the genus Temnothorax or Protomognathus.

KAPOW!

SWISH!

BAM!

CRUNCH! SMACK!

The pirate queen is victorious and leaves with her army and its captives.

ARCHENEMY

Archenemy: Spiders and horned lizards are among the pirate ant's predators. American Museum of Natural History entomologist Christine Johnson, who studies these ants, says horned lizards will sit patiently near a Polyergus nest, watching and waiting for the ants to come out.

Common Name: Siafu ant

Aliases: Driver ant, safari ant

Super-Scientific Name: Dorylus nigricans

Trademark Features: Blackish-brown body, powerful jaws

JAWS OF DOOM!

Size: Queens can be 50-60 mm or even longer, males about 30 mm, and smaller workers as small as half a centimeter.

Secret Hideout: Forests in East Africa and Asia

Superpower: Supersharp jaws

Favorite Food: Earthworms, insects, small reptiles, and mammals

Allies: Dorylus nigricans is part of a large group of Siafu ants within the genus Dorylus, in Africa and Asia. They're also related to the Ecitoninae subfamily of army ants in the Americas.

The **Siafu ant**, or driver ant, may be the most feared insect in Africa and Asia, thanks to its powerful, scissor-like jaws.

CLICK!

CRUNCH!

SNAP!

These ants travel in **huge groups**, marching **by the millions** in search of food. They are known for **eating every living thing in their path**—from insects and earthworms to frogs and mice. There have even been reports of Siafu ants attacking larger mammals that don't get out of their way fast enough. With large prey—like cattle—the ants **swarm into the animal's nose and mouth**, asphyxiating it. Once it's dead, they use their **razor-sharp jaws** to cut it into pieces and carry it back to the nest to eat later.

SLASH! **SWISH!** **CHOMP!**

Archenemy: The honey badger, mongoose, gorilla, and chimpanzee all prey on Siafu ants. Chimps have been observed using tools to feast on these ants in their nests. The chimps break open the nest, then snap a long shoot off a tree and use it as a dipping wand. When the angry ants swarm out of their nest, they start climbing the wand. The chimp grabs the ants, pops them into its mouth, and chews very quickly—before the ants have an opportunity to bite.

ARCHENEMY

The jaws of the Siafu ant are **so powerful** that they hold tight even if the **ant's body is ripped in half.** As a result, people from at least one African tribe have been known to use this ant as a **suture for wounds.** They press the ant's mandibles to a small wound so that the jaws are on either side of the gash. Once the ant bites, they break off its body. The jaws stay clamped shut, closing the wound.

Could super insects take over the world someday?

Maybe! If you've ever wandered outside on a summer night, you know that insects are all around us— crawling through the grass, burrowing in the dirt, and flying through the air. Scientists have identified and named more than nine hundred thousand species of insects on earth and believe that millions more have yet to be discovered. Insects make up three-quarters of the known species on earth, and for every human on the planet, there are at least a million ants. We truly live in a world of bugs. All of them are interesting; a handful are downright incredible.

Some insects have superpowers to rival those of fiction's greatest caped crime fighters. Sure, Superman can fly and stop speeding freight trains, but can he build impossible-to-escape traps like an antlion? Can he shoot glue out his nose like a termite or disguise himself as a flower like an orchid mantis?

The eighteen insect superheroes (and supervillains!) profiled in this book have powers that seem like something out of a comic book. But all of these insects are real, and the information you read on the profile pages is nonfiction—100 percent true.

LIBRARY OF CONGRESS CATALOGING-IN-PUBLICATION DATA.

NAMES: MESSNER, KATE, AUTHOR. | NICKELL, JILLIAN, ILLUSTRATOR.
TITLE: INSECT SUPERPOWERS / BY KATE MESSNER ; ILLUSTRATED BY JILLIAN NICKELL.
DESCRIPTION: SAN FRANCISCO, CALIFORNIA : CHRONICLE BOOKS, LLC, [2019] |
INCLUDES BIBLIOGRAPHICAL REFERENCES.
IDENTIFIERS: LCCN 2017030743| ISBN 9781452139104 | ISBN 1452139105
SUBJECTS: LCSH: INSECTS—JUVENILE LITERATURE. | INSECTS—ADAPTATION—JUVENILE
LITERATURE. | INSECTS—BEHAVIOR—JUVENILE LITERATURE. | ADAPTATION
(BIOLOGY)—JUVENILE LITERATURE.
CLASSIFICATION: LCC QL467.2 .M475 2018 | DDC 595.7—DC23 LC RECORD AVAILABLE AT
HTTPS://LCCN.LOC.GOV/2017030743

MANUFACTURED IN CHINA.

DESIGN BY RYAN HAYES AND JAY MARVEL.
TYPESET IN CC HEDGE BACKWARDS.
THE ILLUSTRATIONS IN THIS BOOK WERE RENDERED IN INK AND COPIC MARKER.

10 9 8 7 6 5 4 3 2 1

CHRONICLE BOOKS LLC
680 SECOND STREET
SAN FRANCISCO, CALIFORNIA 94107

CHRONICLE BOOKS—WE SEE THINGS DIFFERENTLY. BECOME PART OF OUR
COMMUNITY AT WWW.CHRONICLEKIDS.COM.

CHRONICLE BOOKS AND GIFTS ARE AVAILABLE AT SPECIAL QUANTITY
DISCOUNTS TO CORPORATIONS, PROFESSIONAL ASSOCIATIONS,
LITERACY PROGRAMS, AND OTHER ORGANIZATIONS. FOR DETAILS AND
DISCOUNT INFORMATION, PLEASE CONTACT OUR PREMIUMS DEPARTMENT
AT CORPORATESALES@CHRONICLEBOOKS.COM OR AT 1-800-759-0190.

For Gayle Roy-Collin and the readers of
Cumberland Head Elementary School

—K. M.

For Sunny and Joe

—J. N.

If you'd like to learn more about cool insects, check out the following books and online resources:

Albee, Sarah. *Bugged: How Insects Changed History. New York: Walker Books for Young Readers, an imprint of Bloomsbury, 2014.*

Aston, Dianna Hutts. *A Butterfly Is Patient. San Francisco: Chronicle Books, 2011.*

Griffin, Loree. *Citizen Scientists: Be Part of a Scientific Discovery in Your Own Backyard. New York: Henry Holt, 2012.*

Jenkins, Steve. *The Beetle Book. Boston: Houghton Mifflin Harcourt, 2012.*

Johnson, Rebecca L. *Zombie Makers: True Stories of Nature's Undead. Minneapolis: Millbrook Press, 2013.*

Montgomery, Heather. *How Rude: Real Bugs Who Won't Mind Their Manners. New York: Scholastic, 2015.*

Murawski, Darlyne. *Ultimate Bugopedia: The Most Complete Bug Reference Ever. Washington D.C.: National Geographic, 2013.*

Arthropods: The San Diego Zoo.

http://kids.sandiegozoo.org/animals/insects

Bugs: National Geographic.

http://animals.nationalgeographic.com/animals/bugs/